Specifiers' Handbooks for Inclusive Design

Architectural Ironmongery

This guide has been produced by the Centre for Accessible Environments in conjunction with RIBA Enterprises.

Text and drawings by Alison Grant MA Arch RIBA NRAC Consultant
Case studies researched and compiled by Paul Highman

Published: April 2005

ISBN 1 85946 170 0
Stock Code 37722

Centre for Accessible Environments
70 South Lambeth Road
London SW8 1RL

Tel/textphone: +44 (0)20 7840 0125
Fax: +44 (0)20 7840 5811
Email: info@cae.org.uk
Website: www.cae.org.uk

The Centre for Accessible Environments is a Company Limited by Guarantee registered in England and Wales No 3112684, Registered Charity No 1050820.

RIBA Enterprises
15 Bonhill Street
London EC2P 2EA

Tel: +44 (0)20 7496 8300
Fax: +44 (0)20 7374 8200
Email: sales@ribabooks. com
Website: www.ribabookshops.com

RIBA Enterprises is a Company Limited by Guarantee registered in England and Wales No 978271.

Designed by Steve Paveley Design
Typeset by Academic + Technical Typesetting, Bristol
Printed and bound by Latimer Trend, Plymouth

Foreword

The Guild of Architectural Ironmongers, representing some 95 per cent of architectural ironmongers in the UK, is pleased to be able to cooperate with the Centre for Accessible Environments in the production of this important new *Specifiers' Handbooks for Inclusive Design – Architectural Ironmongery*.

The Guild has been an active participant in the preparation of the new European Standards for Ironmongery, which have now been introduced into the UK, and, where applicable, they are referred to in this handbook.

The rights of individuals to have free movement in a building has long been an issue that has been fully supported by the Guild, and through its Registered Architectural Ironmonger scheme it has been advising designers, specifiers and other industry professionals on the best type of equipment to use and its suitability for any given purpose.

The Guild is therefore delighted to have been given the opportunity to support the production of this Design Guide as it contains the latest most up-to-date guidance that is available.

Finally, as there is still some uncertainty about the validity of some of the existing data relating to 'visual contrast', as it applies to architectural ironmongery, the Guild has commissioned further research from the Research Group for Inclusive Environments (RGIE) into specific problems visually impaired people may have in locating door hardware. The outcome of this research is expected to be available in June 2005.

The Guild recommends that you refer to its website www.gai.org.uk for the latest information and updates, or speak to a Registered Architectural Ironmonger, who will be fully conversant with all the relevant legislation and will be able to advise on the best solutions that will enable your building to perform safely and to the satisfaction of all users.

Graham Shirville Reg AI FRSA
Vice Chairman
GAI Technical Committee

Acknowledgements

We are grateful to the Guild of Architectural Ironmongers for sponsorship of this handbook.

Acknowledgements are also due to the following companies who provided photographic illustrations:

Allgood plc
Dorma UK Ltd
Laidlaw
Royde and Tucker Ltd
Turnquest UK Ltd
Winlock
Zero International

Contents

The legislative framework   2

Building Regulations

Architectural ironmongery may be installed as an integral part of a new development, or where improvements are being made to existing buildings. All new developments are subject to approval under the Building Regulations, in which case the provisions in the relevant Approved Document, Technical Standard or Technical Booklet will be applicable. Depending on the nature and extent of building improvements, approval under the Building Regulations may or may not be required.

England and Wales

Approved Document M 2004 Edition *Access to and use of buildings* (AD M) incorporates provisions relating to the installation of architectural ironmongery for manually operated non-powered entrance doors and for internal doors. These provisions cover general aspects of the usability of door handles, visual contrast, and the effect of surface temperature. The appropriate use of self-closing devices, electromagnetic hold-open and swing-free devices is also covered.

Approved Document B *Fire Safety* (AD B) includes provisions for the protection of escape routes and doors on escape routes. Criteria for fire-resisting doors are covered, as are door fastenings and the use of self-closing devices and automatic release mechanisms. In AD B, a self-closing device is specifically defined as 'a device which is capable of closing the door from any angle and against any latch fitted to the door'.

Scotland

The new Technical Handbooks, which come into force in Scotland in May 2005, cover the performance requirements of fire-resisting doors, with reference to emergency exit hardware, door-closing devices and hold-open devices incorporating a fusible link and automatic release mechanisms. No specific mention is made in any section of the Technical Handbooks to other aspects of architectural ironmongery.

Northern Ireland

Technical Booklet E *Fire Safety* covers the performance requirements of fire-resisting doors, with reference to door-closing devices and hold-open devices incorporating a fusible link and automatic release mechanisms.

Technical Booklet R *Access and facilities for disabled people* does not specifically cover any aspect of architectural ironmongery.

A more detailed discussion of the Building Regulations is included in the Appendices.

Disability Discrimination Act 1995

Architectural ironmongery is considered to be a 'physical feature' under the Act. The installation of a particular type of ironmongery, or the provision of supplementary door furniture, may be proposed to overcome an existing barrier to access: for example the provision of a horizontal rail to assist opening or closing of swing doors, or the installation of electromagnetic hold-open devices to fire-resisting doorsets on a corridor route. In this situation, the replacement or provision of additional ironmongery will constitute a 'physical adjustment', designed to remove existing or potential barriers and promote equitable access. Conversely, the inappropriate location of a door handle or the inappropriate use of self-closing devices may itself create a physical barrier. In these situations it may be appropriate for employers, service providers and providers of post-16 education to consider making adjustments to remove or alter the barrier, as a response to their duties under the Act.

The extent and nature of any adjustment will depend on the particular characteristics of the door and ironmongery and on other factors such as practicality, the extent of disruption, the effectiveness of the adjustment, and cost. The duty is to make **reasonable** adjustments, having taken into account all the relevant factors.

Duties under the DDA not only relate to the adjustment of physical features. They also relate to policies, practices and procedures, all of which could have a significant effect on the accessibility and usability of architectural ironmongery. For example, a service provider may have decided to install a self-closing device to the door of the accessible WC because, for the sake of appearances, they do not want the door to be left open when a person exits. However, the self-closing device makes the door extremely heavy to open and presents a barrier to many disabled people attending the building and using the WC facilities. The service provider, in this scenario, is likely to be responding to their duties under the DDA if they remove the self-closing device. To help to ensure the door closes when the WC is vacated, they could install rising-butt hinges.

The DDA does not place duties on product designers and manufacturers in relation to the type of products, packaging or instructions they offer, on the basis that they do not involve the provision of a 'service' direct to the general public. Designers and manufacturers themselves have no duties under the Act to produce, for example, door handles which are suitable for disabled customers. However, employers, service providers and education providers who are responding to their duties to make reasonable adjustments will want to procure products and equipment that are designed to maximise accessibility and meet the needs of a broad range of people. Manufacturers of products such as architectural ironmongery will clearly be designing products and controls suitable for disabled people, albeit on a market-led basis.

Further details on the Disability Discrimination Act 1995 are included in the Appendices.

Construction Products Regulations

The UK Construction Products Regulations (CPR) require construction products to be safe when incorporated into a building. The Regulations have six categories, two of which apply to architectural ironmongery:

- safety in case of fire
- safety in use

All products supplied to a building which is subject to Building Regulations have to satisfy the requirements contained in these Regulations.

Compliance with these regulations can be most easily demonstrated by producers CE Marking their products. Although CE Marking is not a mandatory requirement in the UK it is in most other EU countries, and many producers are already following this route.

CE Marking

CE Marking is the manufacturer's declaration that the product meets the requirements of relevant European Directives as implemented by national legislation such as the CPR. CE Marking in relation to architectural ironmongery verifies that:

- the product meets the requirements of the Construction Products Regulations

- that it has been satisfactorily tested by a third party to verify standards established by a relevant harmonised European Standard
- there is the required level of factory production control at the manufacturing facilities, and that this is subject to regular third-party checks

CE Marking can only be applied to products that are within the scope of the standards marked with an asterisk overleaf.

Introduction

Specifiers' Handbooks series

The *Specifiers' Handbooks for Inclusive Design* series comprises a set of design guides which look in detail at the technical aspects of key building elements. The series expands on guidance in *Designing for Accessibility*, a leading CAE/RIBA Enterprises publication covering inclusive design in a range of public buildings.

The *Specifiers' Handbooks for Inclusive Design* series has been prepared to assist designers, specifiers, building owners and occupiers, building managers and facilities managers to understand key design aspects and characteristics of specific architectural elements. The series combines technical guidance with informative case studies, designed to facilitate a practical understanding of the element in focus. The first three handbooks in the series cover:

- Platform lifts
- Architectural ironmongery
- Automatic door systems

The information in the handbooks should assist people responsible for the selection and specification of each architectural element to make decisions which will lead to the procurement of the most suitable product.

The information will also assist people who are responsible for ongoing maintenance to understand the importance of regular checks and the implications for disabled and other people if equipment is taken out of action for any reason.

About this handbook

Architectural Ironmongery covers detailed aspects of door ironmongery, including manually-operated door handles, locks, latches, self-closing devices, pull handles, door thresholds, door protection, window fittings and some specialist ironmongery.

The handbook offers practical guidance to help specifiers understand the different types of architectural ironmongery available, the factors contributing to the design and specification, and related legislation, building regulations and standards. The design guidance is supported by case study examples which illustrate different types of ironmongery in a range of situations.

An increasing number of doors are now being fitted with automatic door systems to provide easier access through heavier doors and to the main entrance doors of public buildings. These systems are covered in detail in another handbook in the series: *Automatic Door Systems*.

The publication of the revised Approved Document M to the Building Regulations for England and Wales, which came into effect in May 2004, presented a number of challenges to ironmongery professionals and manufacturers, designers, clients and building control officials. Revisions to the document relating to the provision of ironmongery to doors located on accessible routes were considerable and in many cases differed from existing procedures and the guidance provided by BS 8300:2001 and a number of other documents.

Since the issue of the revised Approved Document M, a number of task groups, comprising industry and client representatives, have met to consider the implications of the differing guidance. Several consultation meetings have also been held with personnel from the Office of the Deputy Prime Minister (ODPM), the department responsible for drafting all Approved Documents.

During the second half of 2004, the British Standards Institution (BSI) committee responsible for BS 8300 agreed to produce a set of amendments to the 2001 edition of this standard and these will be issued during 2005 in advance of a full revision which will be published later.

Many of the amendments being made to BS 8300 have been incorporated into a Frequently Asked Questions (FAQ) page concerning Approved Document M on the Building Regulations section of the ODPM website www.odpm.gov.uk. By this route the two documents will be usefully aligned and provide non-conflicting advice.

This *Specifiers' Handbook* incorporates these 2005 amendments.

Design and specification guidelines

British and European Standards

A number of British and European Standards are applicable to the selection, installation and use of architectural ironmongery, the most relevant being:

- BS 8214:1990 *Code of practice for fire door assemblies with non-metallic leaves*
- BS 8424: 2003 *Building hardware – Pull handles – Requirements and test methods*
- BS EN 179: 1998 *Building hardware – Emergency exit devices operated by a lever handle or push pad – Requirements and test methods**
- BS EN 1125: 1997 *Building hardware – Panic exit devices operated by horizontal bar – Requirements and test methods**
- BS EN 1154:1997 *Building hardware – Controlled door closing devices – Requirements and test methods**
- BS EN 1155:1997 *Building hardware – Electrically powered hold-open devices for swing doors – Requirements and test methods**
- BS EN 1906:2002 *Building hardware – Lever handles and knob furniture – Requirements and test methods*
- BS EN 1935:2002 *Building hardware – Single-axis hinges – Requirements and test methods**
- BS EN 12209:2003 *Building hardware – Locks and latches – Mechanically operated locks, latches and locking plates – Requirements and test methods**

* Indicates a harmonised standard which permits CE Marking of the products where they are placed on the market for use on fire-resisting and escape route doors.

Another relevant British Standard is BS 8300:2001 *Design of buildings and their approaches to meet the needs of disabled people – Code of practice*. This document explains how the built environment can be designed to anticipate and overcome restrictions that prevent disabled people from making full use of premises and their surroundings.

Many of the design recommendations in BS 8300 are based for the first time on ergonomic research commissioned in 1997 and 2001 by the Department of the Environment, Transport and the Regions. BS 8300 includes commentary which provides a context and rationale for the design guidance. Management and maintenance issues are incorporated, in recognition that these play an essential part in the delivery of accessible services and facilities to disabled people.

The recommendations in the standard apply to car parking provision, setting-down points and garaging, access routes to and around all buildings, and entrances to and interiors of new buildings. They inform the design guidance in AD M of the Building Regulations. They may also be used to assess the accessibility and usability of existing buildings and, where practicable, as a basis for their improvement.

As noted in the introduction, a set of amendments to BS 8300 will be issued by BSI during 2005, some of which relate to the provision of architectural ironmongery.

Design issues

Architectural ironmongery comprises a range of components which facilitate the correct functioning of a door or window opening. Components such as hinges, locks and door closers are functional devices which provide for door movement, security and mechanical closing. Other components such as handles and rails provide the interface with the person using the door and, as such, must be designed to provide for easy and comfortable use of the door.

The effort required to open and fully close any door depends on natural and designed environmental conditions in addition to the functional characteristics of all door components. Natural air flows, air conditioning and mechanical ventilation systems create air pressure differentials which can significantly alter the force required to open the door. Hinge friction, the resistance of latches, the use of door seals for environmental or fire safety performance and, of course, the force exerted by any mechanical door-closing devices, can all contribute to an increase in the opening force.

Accurate and appropriate specification of all components of a door is therefore essential and should be undertaken with regard to the door location and surrounding environmental conditions.

Visual contrast

Door furniture, pull handles, rails and push plates on accessible routes should always contrast visually with the door surface to improve identification by visually impaired people.

Approved Document M 2004 (England and Wales) includes provisions for visual contrast, which it defines as a difference in the light reflectance value (LRV) between surfaces of greater than 30 points. The LRV represents how much useful light is reflected from a surface, with higher value LRVs indicating a higher level of reflectance.

The 2005 amendments to BS 8300 acknowledge that the research-based evidence for the 30 point figure is limited and that anecdotal evidence suggests a 20 points difference in LRVs may be acceptable in certain circumstances. The current view is that adjacent larger surfaces such as walls and floors may not require a 30 point difference in LRVs in order to provide

Effective visual contrast improves identification of the door ironmongery

adequate visual contrast. It is more important that smaller objects positioned against a large background, such as a lever handle viewed against a door leaf, achieve effective visual contrast, represented by a higher point difference in LRVs. A LRV difference of less than 20 points may not achieve adequate visual contrast for any combination of surfaces or objects. The AD M FAQ page on the ODPM website also refers to '20 points'.

The amendments to BS 8300 also acknowledge that there is little research-based information concerning the influence of different surface textures or of the impact (good or bad) on the use of reflective finishes for items such as door handles.

Aside from the use of extreme contrast between elements, such as black door handles on a white door leaf, how can a satisfactory level of LRV difference be assessed and achieved in practice?

Two types of equipment are available, albeit not currently in regular use outside test laboratories and research institutions. The most sophisticated piece of equipment is a spectrophotometer which is able to measure both flat and curved surfaces with matt, metallic and reflective finishes. The alternative hand-held colorimeter provides a means of assessing LRVs on site using a comparative high-reflectance standard surface. Approximate LRVs can be established using a colorimeter by comparing the luminance of the standard surface with the surface being assessed, as long as the luminance of each is measured under the same lighting conditions. Colorimeters cannot be used to measure curved surfaces or gloss finishes.

Of more relevance to the majority of designers and specifiers is the use of swatch samples for surface finishes and products on which LRVs are defined by the manufacturers. The difference between LRVs in an existing environment can be approximated by comparison with matching swatch samples for which the LRVs are known. This method has its limitations – LRVs established in this way are dependent on the ambient lighting and do not account for influence of glossy finishes. Nonetheless, once LRV information is available for a wide enough range of components, designers should be better equipped to select products, surface finishes and colours which will achieve the recommended degree of visual contrast.

The Guild of Architectural Ironmongers, with financial support from its membership, has commissioned the Research Group for Inclusive Environments (RGIE) to undertake research to assess the ability of people with a visual impairment to easily locate door ironmongery. The research will examine the effects of LRV differences between the door surface finish and ironmongery and in relation to gloss levels. The research will use actual samples of ironmongery viewed at a range of approximately one metre. This should simulate, as far as possible, the real use of these items. The results of this research are expected to be available in June 2005.

Door opening and closing forces

The guidance relating to door opening and closing forces has been subject to some

discrepancy, in particular between a number of British and European Standards, the requirements of the Construction Products Regulations, CE Marking requirements and the guidance in Approved Documents B and M (England and Wales). The provisions in AD M referred to a maximum **opening force** of 20 newtons for doors on accessible routes. This force, however, was approximately 50 per cent lower than the level typically achieved on doors fitted with new self-closing devices and, up until recently, generally accepted as the norm. The provision of self-closing devices meeting the 20 newton maximum opening force while also meeting the requirements of CE Marking to BS EN 1154 (required for fire-resisting doors) has been virtually impossible.

Until now, BS 8300 guidance for fire-resisting doors fitted with a self-closing device refers to a maximum **closing force** of 20 newtons. Above this level, fire-resisting doors are recommended to have an electrically powered hold-open device to avoid the need for the door to be opened manually.

The amendments to BS 8300 and the AD M FAQ page on the ODPM website now indicate that self-closing devices fitted to single swing doors should have 'controlled' action and conform to the requirements of BS EN 1154. The revised guidance quotes a maximum **opening force** of 30 newtons when measured between 0 and 30 degrees open and 22.5 newtons when measured between 30 and 60 degrees open. The opening force limits relate to measurements taken at the leading edge of the door.

The reason that the maximum opening force is required to reduce once the door is past the initial stage of opening is that people generally find it easier to open a door past the initial force of the closer but experience difficulty once the door is past the 30 degree position.

Opening forces can be measured on site using a plunger-type force measuring instrument. Wherever possible, the force should be measured from the leading edge of the door. However, the style of measuring instrument and design of the door may preclude this, in which case measurements should be taken in line with the pivot of any lever handle or along the centre line of a push plate, so long as this is no more than 60mm from the leading edge. If this is the case, the opening force limits given above may be increased by 2 newtons.

When taking site measurements of door opening forces, the inherent limitations of the measuring equipment and site conditions should be taken into account as they may result in variations in the results of 2–3 newtons.

Non-fire-resisting doors, which are required to self-close for reasons of privacy, acoustics or energy control, should be fitted with controlled door-closing devices selected, fitted and adjusted so that the opening forces are well below the limits set out above.

Technical guidelines

Hinges

Hinges carry the full mass of a door and must also be sufficient to take any extra load exerted by a person leaning on the door or door furniture for support. Low-friction hinges are essential to minimise the opening and closing forces and also to resist wear. The selection of appropriate hinges for the door size and mass is paramount and, typically, three hinges per leaf will be required. Two of these hinges should normally be positioned towards the top of the door, where they can take the lateral load of a swinging door unless other locations are required by fire test evidence.

BS EN 1935 gives guidance on the grades of hinges available and the maximum permitted friction. High-performance hinges are available which contribute less than 1 newton friction to door movement.

- Low-friction hinges should be used to improve door swing and minimise opening and closing forces.
- The type, number and position of hinges should be determined by the door size and weight.
- Rising butt hinges can be used to help keep a door 'closed to'. This may be beneficial

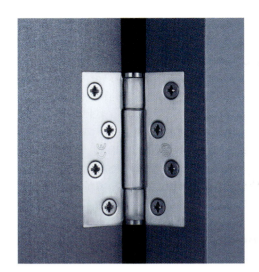

Low-friction hinges improve door swing and reduce opening and closing forces

where there is a risk of an open door presenting a hazard, for example to blind and partially sighted people.
- Pivot hinges can be used in conjunction with an emergency release bolt on doors such as accessible WC doors, which ordinarily open inwards, but which are required to open outwards in an emergency. See also section *Specialist ironmongery* p 19.
- The use of swing-clear hinges could be considered in order to maximise the clear opening width of a door. Swing-clear hinges align the door leaf with the door stop when open to 90 degrees, and thereby reduce the projection of door handles into the opening space.

Double-action floor springs are recessed below the floor finish

Door furniture

The term 'door furniture' in this handbook refers to door handles, bolt, lock and latch mechanisms. Pull handles and rails are covered in the section to follow.

The provision of well-designed door furniture that is easy to use and suitably positioned will greatly improve accessibility. Selection of the most appropriate type of door furniture will depend on the function of the door, latching and security measures and aesthetics.

The use of door knobs should be avoided as they are difficult to grip and turn, particularly for people with reduced manual dexterity. Door knobs typically require a greater force to operate a latch than a lever handle and are also difficult to use if the hand is wet.

Lever handles offer a more suitable and usable alternative to operate lock and latch mechanisms. Lever handles are typically operated by gripped hands or fingers, but can also be used with the palm of the hand, forearm or elbow. The 'lever action' provides an efficient way of overcoming the resistance of the spring in the latch mechanism and lever handle assembly.

Where latched doors are required to be locked, the keyway should be unobstructed so that it is easily identified by people with visual impairments, and accessible to people with reduced manual dexterity.

Latches contribute to the force required to close a door and should be carefully specified. High-performance latches are available which contribute resistance of less than 5 newtons to the required closing force. BS EN 12209 sets out detailed guidance on the resistance classes of latches.

BS EN 1906 sets out detailed requirements for the performance and strength of lever handles and BS 8424 for pull handles.

- Door lever handles should be positioned between 900mm and 1100mm above floor or ground level. A height of 1000mm is preferred.
- Doors fitted with a latch should be capable of being operated using a closed fist. This can be best achieved using a lever handle.
- Lever handles are available in a wide range of profiles and styles, some of which are easier to use than others. Lever handles should be comfortable to hold and operate.
- Lever handles which have a round-bar profile with a diameter of 19mm minimum and a clearance of 45mm from the back of the handle to the door face are considered to be the easiest to use, but are not the only acceptable style.
- Lever handles which incorporate a return end are preferred as these are often more

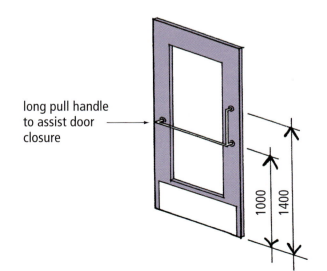

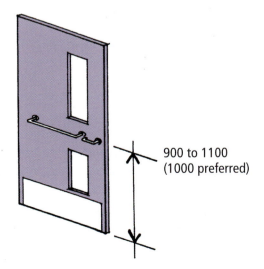

Figure 1 **Height of door handles**

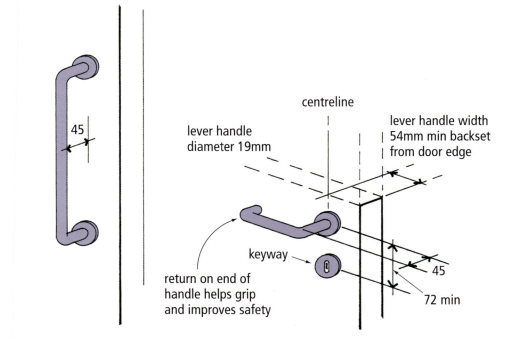

centreline

lever handle
diameter 19mm

lever handle width
54mm min backset
from door edge

keyway

return on end of
handle helps grip
and improves safety

45

45

72 min

Figure 2 **Door handle details**

comfortable to hold and reduce the risk of clothing or straps from bags being caught by the handle (see *Figure 2*).

- The cylinder to a mortice lock/latch should be either located above the lever handle or a minimum vertical distance of 72mm between the keyway and handle.
- All door furniture should be securely fixed, preferably with bolt-through fixings – these are much stronger than single-side or surface fixings. The strength and durability of door furniture is particularly important as a person may lean on a handle or rail for support.
- The proximity of a lever handle to any vision panel beading should be carefully considered. Perimeter beading, particularly timber beading, may project from the door face and graze the hand or arm as the lever is depressed. This should be avoided by careful design and specification.
- Locks should be carefully selected to ensure ease of operation for all building users. Thumb-turn locks and small levers should be avoided as these can be particularly difficult for people with reduced manual dexterity to operate.
- All door furniture should contrast visually with the surface of the door (see section above).

- The position and style of door furniture throughout a building should be consistent.
- Handles on the external face of entrance doors should not be cold to the touch. This can be best achieved using plastic, nylon-coated or timber surfaces. Bare metal surfaces should be avoided.
- Keys with a large 'bow' may be beneficial to people with reduced manual dexterity or strength as they reduce the effect of the force required to engage the dead bolt. Some keys can be fitted with bow adaptors.
- If door bolts are required to be accessible, consider the use of extended arm bolts.

Pull handles and rails

Doors which are not required to be latched or locked are usually fitted with pull handles. Pull handles are commonly used for doors along circulation routes which are fitted with self-closing devices, or to lobby doors.

Full-height tubular handles provide a handle that can be easily used by people at a range of heights, which is a good feature. However, the size and position of the handle may restrict the effective clear opening width of the door, and

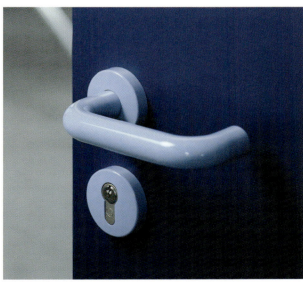

Doors fitted with mechanical door-closing devices or low-energy operators are typically fitted with pull handles for manual operation

this should be taken into account when determining the door size and structural width.

Where doors do not have self-closing devices, the provision of a horizontal rail in addition to lever handles assists door opening and enables wheelchair users in particular to pull doors closed behind them.

- Pull handles should be positioned vertically with the lower end 1000mm above floor or ground level and be 400mm in length. The recommended clearance from the handle to the door face is 45mm (see *Figure 2*).
- An additional horizontal rail should be provided on the push side of the door, 1000mm above floor level, to assist door closing. This is particularly relevant where doors do not have self-closing devices.
- Where self-closing double-action 'swing' doors are installed (that is, where a door can be pushed open from both sides) it may still be preferable for pull handles to be provided. This enables the door to be opened by a person on one side of the door, out of courtesy and/or to provide assistance, for a person approaching on the other side. Pushing a door open towards another person is not always practical owing to limitations in space, and may compromise safety.
- As with the recommendations for lever handles, pull handles and rails should

Lever handles are available in a wide range of styles and finishes. They should be selected to promote ease of use and effective visual contrast

contrast visually with the surface of the door.

- Handles on the external face of entrance doors should be of a material that is not cold to the touch. This can be best achieved using plastic, nylon-coated or timber surfaces. Bare metal surfaces should be avoided.

Door control

Door control devices include mechanical and/or electrically powered devices which close a door after it has been opened manually, electromagnetic hold-open devices, swing-free devices and low-energy power-assisted door operators.

Door-closing devices are mechanical devices which close a door (both single and double action) after it has been opened manually. They are used widely, particularly in public buildings and in the workplace. Their use is essential on most fire-resisting and smoke control doors. Many external entrance doors require a closing device to reduce heat loss from the building. Security considerations may also require doors to be self-closing.

Selection of the most appropriate type of door-closing device will depend on the door size, type, location, expected traffic and performance requirements. Suitability of the door closer will also depend on whether an automatic fire detection and alarm system is installed in the building. Where such a system is installed, the opportunity is available to provide integral hold-open and closing devices which enable doors to be held open in normal use, or swing-free devices which allow the door to be left at any angle, but close if the alarm is activated, thereby maintaining safety in the event of a fire. In smaller buildings where there is no automatic fire detection and alarm system, only mechanical closing devices are accepted by the Fire Authorities.

Differential air pressures within a building can affect door movements and can also increase the force required to open a door, irrespective of the setting of any door-closing device. The selection of a suitable closing device should

Surface-mounted hydraulic door-closing device

therefore be undertaken with full consideration to the complete door system comprising the door leaf and frame, hinges, seals and latches and any differential air pressures.

The over-use of door closers can create a significant barrier to the ease of movement of people around a building and should be avoided. Door-closing devices should only be used where there is a need to conserve heat (for example, a main entrance door), for security, and where there is a mandatory requirement, such as for fire-resisting doors.

Mechanical door-closing devices

Adjustable-strength hydraulic door-closing devices – These devices operate on a rack and pinion or cam-action principle and incorporate a spring coil (or coils). Both the closing speed and the closing/opening force can be adjusted to suit the particular door width and operating conditions.

These door closers can be surface mounted at the head of the door, concealed within the door leaf or transom, or concealed within the floor as floor springs. Where doors are required to be double-action, door closers are most commonly concealed within the transom or floor.

- Door-closing devices can incorporate a backcheck which is a cushioning action designed to prevent the door from being pushed wide open at speed. The backcheck should come into effect at an angle not less than 80 degrees.

A hydraulic door-closer mechanism concealed within the door leaf and frame can improve the aesthetics of the door

- A **delayed action** facility enables door closure to be delayed by allowing the door to remain open for an adjustable period of time before closing at a pre-set speed. This feature is beneficial to people who may move slowly through the door opening.
- Door-closing devices can be used in conjunction with electromagnetic hold-open devices (see section on *Electrically powered door hold-open devices* p 15).
- The speed of double-action doors should be adjusted so that they do not swing back past the closed position, as this can be hazardous for a person moving slowly through the door opening.
- The maximum closing force of any self-closing device should be within 0 and 15 degrees of final closure.
- In order not to exceed the 30 newton opening force limit on self-closing fire doors it will be necessary to use selected 'high efficiency' closing devices that are CE Marked to BS EN1154 in conjunction with low-friction hinges or pivots, and, where fitted, latch bolts and seals.
- Without regular maintenance of all architectural ironmongery, opening and closing forces can increase to the extent that independent access is difficult or impossible for some disabled people. Verification of the opening forces described above should be covered in an access statement and building maintenance plan.

Fixed-strength hydraulic door-closing devices – These devices operate in a similar way to the adjustable type, but the closing/opening force cannot be adjusted on site. Therefore, if an inappropriate device has been installed, it will often be necessary to fit a complete replacement.

Spring door-closing devices – These are relatively basic door-closing springs and have no means of controlling either the speed or force of door closing. These devices are not recommended as their use can lead to fire doors not closing correctly. They close the door in an uncontrolled manner, which is dangerous for users; they can also be noisy in operation and cause damage to the door frame.

Electrically powered door hold-open devices

An electrically powered hold-open device is a device fitted to a door that enables the door to either swing free or be held firmly in the open position, and which closes the door when the electrical power is released. Such devices can be used in buildings which have a fully automatic fire alarm system installed and in locations where a closing device is required

A separate free-standing magnet can be fixed to the door leaf and wall surface or floor box

for safety reasons, such as a fire-resisting door, but where it is preferable for the door to be held in the open position for ease of access. Electromagnetic hold-open devices are often used along corridor routes where there may be one or more fire-resisting doors, all required to be self-closing. Travel along the corridor is greatly improved if the doors can be held firmly open, but in a manner which ensures integrity of the components in the event of a fire.

Electrically powered door hold-open devices fall into two categories: electromagnetic hold-open devices and swing-free devices.

Electromagnetic hold-open devices – These devices can either be integral units, incorporating both a hold-open and closing mechanism, or separate hold-open devices which can be used in conjunction with individual door-closing devices. Combined units are less likely to be damaged, and provide greater flexibility of the hold-open position. The separate hold-open mechanism typically incorporates electromagnetic plates, one of which is fixed to the door face and one to the adjacent wall or floor box.

- The holding force of any separate mechanism should be selected to suit the power size of the selected door closer and the door mass.

- Hold-open devices should be capable of being released manually. It is preferable for this to be achieved by the provision of an accessible and clearly identified push button, either mounted on the device or close by.
- Free-standing magnets should be fitted as close to the leading edge of the door as possible. This is so that the magnet can exert maximum hold against the door and reduce the likelihood of damage should the door edge be pushed beyond the fully open position.
- Magnets and door closers should always be fixed in the same plane: that is, overhead closers should have magnets fitted towards the top of the door and floor springs should have magnets fitted at floor level. This is to ensure the door is not twisted while being held in the fully open position.
- The hold-open devices should be tested on a regular basis to ensure that they continue to 'fail safe'.

Electromagnetic swing-free devices – These devices enable a door to be used as if there were no closing device fitted: that is, the door leaf can be opened and closed with minimum effort. The swing-free device incorporates a closer arm which moves with the door leaf, but which exerts no closing force as long as the mechanism is 'energised' by a power supply. When the power supply is interrupted, for example when the fire alarm is activated, the closer arm is released and the door is closed under spring power. The unit operates as a

Electromagnetic swing-free devices can look very similar to conventional hydraulic door-closing devices, but enable the door to swing free of control until the power supply is interrupted and the door closes under spring power

normal door closer until the power supply is restored.

Doors fitted with swing-free devices, because they are able to swing free of control, are susceptible to air movement and wind pressures in a building.

• Swing-free units should only be used on inward-opening doors. They are not suitable for use in corridors.

Low-energy door operators

Low-energy swing doors are powered door-opening devices which can also be manually operated. They can be used on internal and external doors in low-traffic areas and in situations where manual operation of the door needs to be retained, with the availability for powered assistance when required.

Low-energy operators have two main methods of operation:

• **power-assisted operation** in which the initiating signal is provided by the action of pushing, pulling or touching the door leaf or handle; or
• **power operation** in which the initiating signal is provided by a manual or automatic activation device. Manual activation devices include wall or

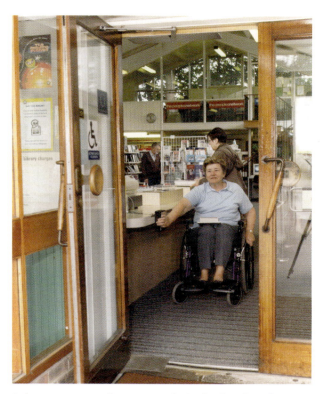

A low-energy door-opening device has been retrofitted to this existing library exit door. The door has a desk-mounted push pad as a manual activation device

post-mounted push pads, swipe card, proximity card and keypad devices. Doors can also be activated using remote control transmitters, which can be hand held or mounted on a wheelchair.

The operating system is accommodated in an overhead box similar to, but much larger than, a conventional door-closing device.

• Manual controls for power-operated doors should be located at a height between 750mm and 1000mm above floor level and set back 1400mm from the leading edge of the door.
• Manual controls should contrast in colour and luminance with the background surfaces so that they are readily identifiable.
• If a door fitted with a low-energy opening device can be approached from the side when the door is in the open position, a safety barrier should be provided.
• If low-energy swing doors are installed on emergency exit routes, the doors should be

Low-energy door-opening devices are mounted at the head of the door and are typically larger than conventional door-closing devices

capable of being manually opened in the direction of escape.

Low-energy door operators are discussed in more detail in *Specifiers' Handbooks for Inclusive Design: Automatic Door Systems*.

Door protection

Doors which can be pushed open, particularly those which require some degree of force to counteract door closers, may sustain some damage to the lower surface of the door leaf from impact by wheelchair footplates and hubs, walking frames or footwear. The integrity and appearance of the door leaf can be protected using kick plates. While the kick plate itself may also sustain damage, it is likely to be made from a more robust material than the door leaf, and can be replaced at a much lower cost.

Push plates which visually contrast with the door leaf help to identify the leading edge of the door

- The recommended size of kick plate is 400mm high by the full width of the door leaf.
- A lower-height kick plate will be necessary for doors with a glazed panel extending below 400mm.
- Highly polished or reflective kick plates should be avoided as they can create the illusion that there is a large gap under the door.
- It is not necessary for the kick plate to contrast visually with the door leaf.

Doors which are required to be pushed open, and have no handles, can be confusing because there are no clues as to which side of the door should be pushed. The addition of a push plate highlights which side of the door forms the leading edge, and also protects the door surface from finger marks.

- Push plates should be provided to the leading edge of all push-only doors which have no other handles.
- Push plates should contrast visually with the door surface so that they are easily identifiable. Highly reflective push plates should be avoided as they may give the illusion of being a vision panel.

Door seals and thresholds

A range of products is available for sealing gaps between the door leaf and frame. Draught seals reduce potential heat loss; threshold seals prevent water ingress; intumescent fire and smoke seals contribute to the integrity of fire-resisting doors; and acoustic seals improve privacy in locations where sound transmission may otherwise present a problem. Seals may also be required in specialist situations to reduce gas and air leakage or to prevent light penetration.

By their very nature, seals increase the resistance between the door leaf and frame and contribute to the force required to open and fully close a door. Compression and swipe seals, in particular, may create friction and prevent a door from closing properly.

Door thresholds to external entrance or exit doors should ideally be level in order to provide

External and internal door thresholds should be as level as possible and incorporate chamfered or pencil-rounded corners. Vertical surfaces should be no greater than 5mm

a convenient means of access and egress for all building users. However, where a small change in level is necessary, for example to bridge the change in level between different existing floor surfaces or to ensure an adequate degree of weather protection, a threshold bar which has a minimal change in level may be used.

Internal door thresholds may, in some circumstances, benefit from the use of door threshold bars, particularly where there is a change in floor finish on each side of the door. A threshold bar will ensure that the edges of flooring materials are firmly secured and prevent potential trip hazards caused by loose or raised edges of carpets, sheet materials or other floor finishes. Internal doors where the floor surface is similar on both sides are unlikely to require threshold bars.

- To minimise door-closing resistance, seals should be carefully selected and installed to a fine tolerance.
- External entrance doors should, ideally, incorporate a level threshold. If a change in level is unavoidable, the threshold should be a maximum height of 15mm, with no vertical edge greater than 5mm. All corners should be chamfered or pencil rounded.
- Where there is a junction between different floor finishes within a door opening, a permanent threshold bar should be provided. The threshold should be level, wherever practicable, or incorporate a chamfered or pencil-rounded upstand where required to bridge the change in level between different floor finishes.

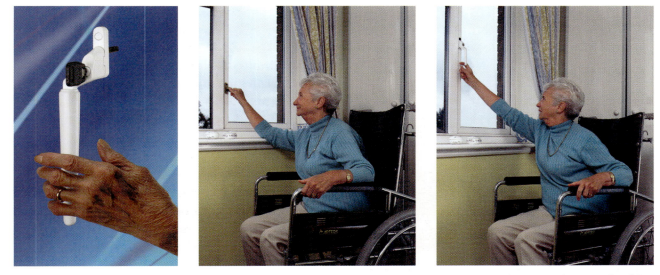

Window handles should be selected for ease of use and positioned where they can be reached in both a closed and an open position

Window fittings

In environments which are naturally ventilated, comfort and convenience for all building users is achieved by windows which can be easily opened. This relies not only on suitable positioning of the window and any opening light, but also on the provision of locks, handles and mechanisms which are easy to use and require minimal force to operate. Where windows themselves may not be easily accessible, the provision or replacement of handles and locking mechanisms with extended-arm handles, rod or pole operation, winding-handle mechanisms or powered window systems may be appropriate. Some examples of window-operating systems available include the following:

- Rod-operated systems enable a lever handle to be mounted at low level on a casement frame which, when activated, disengages a fastener at both low and high level. This system enables the handle to be positioned at a lower level than is normally required for side-hung casement windows.
- Fanlights which are hinged along the bottom edge and open inwards can be fitted with a fanlight catch which can be operated with an extended rod or cord.
- Top-hung and pivot windows can be fitted with a cam-operated or screw rod opener which can be activated by a pole if the window is at high level, or by hand for lower-level windows.
- Flexible cable gear, incorporating a winding handle or electric motor, is commonly used

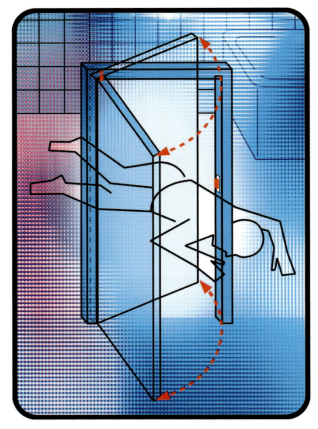

A double-action floor pivot hinge and emergency release bolt enables a door which normally opens into a room to be opened outwards in an emergency

to operate high-level windows which are beyond the range of pole or cord operation. Any winding handles or electric controls should be mounted where they are easily accessible.

Specialist ironmongery

Doors which ordinarily open in one direction only, but which are required to open in the opposite direction in certain situations, can be fitted with a pivot hinge and an emergency release bolt. This situation could arise, for example, in relation to inward-opening doors to wheelchair accessible WCs. (Inward-opening doors may be acceptable if the room is sufficiently large and a clear turning area of at least 1500mm diameter is maintained, clear of the door swing and all sanitaryware.) It is important, however, that the door can be opened outwards in the event that a person falls against the back of the door inside the WC.

Double-action floor pivot hinge and emergency release catch

This can be achieved if a pivot hinge and emergency release bolt are installed. All locks and indicator bolts should incorporate an emergency-release facility.

This combination of ironmongery should not be considered appropriate for day-to-day use, for example as a means of 'getting away with' an inward-opening door to an accessible WC.

Building management

Operation and maintenance

Architectural ironmongery, when installed properly and fully operational, contributes to the correct functioning of a door and convenient use of handles, latches and locks. However, as with many moving components and mechanisms, continued use may cause wear, may cause fixings to loosen (or tighten), and may make the door or hardware difficult to use. In some cases, defective ironmongery will lead to potentially hazardous situations, for example when a self-closing device fails to fully close a fire- or smoke-resisting door.

Doors fitted with electromagnetic hold-open and swing-free devices should be checked for correct operation on a monthly basis.

Other manually operated doors should be inspected at six-monthly intervals in accordance with BS 8214. Regular maintenance helps to ensure that all ironmongery is suitably adjusted and fully operational. Particular attention should be paid to emergency exit hardware, hinges and self-closing devices.

Adjustments should be made to self-closing devices to ensure that the speed and force of door closing is suitable and that the doors close completely and at a safe speed.

Case studies

Horniman Museum

Architect Charles Harrison Townsend designed the Grade II listed Horniman Museum, which opened in 1901, to house a collection of natural history specimens, cultural artefacts and musical instruments for the Victorian tea trader Frederick John Horniman.

In 1999 the Museum demolished some of the later additions to the building and embarked on a Centenary Development to create a new extension and several associated spaces. The new building extension, designed by architects Allies and Morrison, opened in June 2002. The extension provides a new gallery for the musical instrument collection, space to accommodate large touring exhibitions, new education areas, a shop and café.

Allies and Morrison have specified a hard-wearing range of ironmongery which has a clean, minimalist design quality that is not over-styled or over-designed, but has a sufficient range to cover most situations. The brushed stainless steel design integrates with the overall aesthetic of the Museum.

In these larger-than-standard doors, the provision of pull handles at two different heights (left) and extended pull handles (right) helps to ensure the door can be used by people at a range of heights

Disability Rights Commission, London

The Disability Rights Commission (DRC) new London headquarters occupy the third floor of a modern office building in the City. The DRC office was extensively refurbished prior to occupation and equipped with a range of different door systems and furniture to provide easy access throughout the building.

The architects for the refurbishment, Cheyne Swan, specified dark blue nylon-coated steel pull handles, lever handles and escutcheons, with matching hinges, kick plates and push plates. This ironmongery supplements the automatic door controls also installed on many of the doors.

The dark blue colour of the ironmongery (handles, push plates, toilet locks, hooks, hinges and door signs) provides effective visual contrast against the yellow doors.

Where necessary, two sets of locks are used, located at two heights, 1000mm and 600mm above floor level, convenient for people who are walking, and for wheelchair users and those of small stature.

The WC door has been fitted with locks at two heights to suit people with different reach ranges. As the door is outward opening and has no self-closing device, a horizontal rail has been provided on the inside to assist door closing

The dark blue push plates, kick plates, pull handles and accessories provide effective visual contrast with the yellow door leaves and adjacent surfaces

Royal Academy of Dramatic Art

The Royal Academy of Dramatic Art (RADA) celebrated its centenary year with the completion of a new award-winning building in 2000. The new building, designed by Avery Associates Architects, contains three public performance spaces, foyers, café bar, workshops, rehearsal rooms, recording studios, classrooms, offices and back-of-house facilities in a narrow ten-storey building that has been accommodated in RADA's historic site in London's West End. With state-of-the-art theatre spaces, innovatively designed light wells and spectacular curved glass façade to Malet Street, the new building has ironmongery in keeping with its elegant, modern design.

A combination of bespoke and standard ironmongery was specified. Fendor Hanson, door designers, were responsible for the internal glass doors, and specified polished steel full-height pull handles, with textured grip sections. All the metalwork was blasted, weather blocked, primed and polyester powder-coated with a semi-gloss metallic grey finish. The doors have been hung on floor springs with a top-centre pivot.

Full-height steel handrails with integral push and pull rails to both sides

Full-height powder-coated pull handles

Appendices

Building Regulations

England and Wales

In England and Wales, building design and construction is governed by the Building Regulations. These regulations comprise a series of requirements for specific purposes: health and safety, energy conservation, prevention of contamination of water, and the welfare and convenience of persons in or about buildings.

Part M – Part M of the Regulations sets minimum legal standards for access to and use of buildings by all building users, including disabled people. Since a requirement for access was first introduced in 1985, there have been a number of changes to and extensions in the scope of access regulations. The most recent – and most radical – revision came into effect on 1 May 2004. Whereas, previously, Part M was concerned with 'access for disabled people', now the requirement (for non-domestic buildings) is simply that:

- **Access and use**
  'Reasonable provision shall be made for people to gain access to and use the building and its facilities.'

This does not apply to any part of a building that is used solely to enable the building or any service or fitting within the building to be inspected, repaired or maintained.

- **Access to extensions to buildings**
  'Suitable independent access shall be provided to the extension where reasonably practicable.'

This does not apply where suitable access to the extension is provided throughout the building that is extended.

- **Sanitary conveniences in extensions to buildings**
  'If sanitary conveniences are provided in any building that is to be extended, reasonable provision shall be made within the extension for sanitary conveniences.'

This does not apply where there is reasonable provision for sanitary conveniences elsewhere in the building that can be accessed by building users.

The regulation avoids specific reference to, and a definition of, disabled people. This inclusive approach means that buildings and their facilities should be accessible to and usable by all people who use buildings – including parents with children, older people and disabled people. Previously, Part M covered new buildings and extensions to existing buildings. The 2004 revision brings Part M into line with other parts of the Building Regulations by extending its scope to include alterations to existing buildings and certain changes of use.

Approved Document M – Building Regulations are supported by 'Approved Documents' which give practical guidance with respect to the regulations. While their use is not mandatory – and the requirements of regulations can be met in other ways – Approved Documents are used as a benchmark by the building control authority. The new Approved Document M (AD M), published in November 2003, offers technical guidance on providing access to and within buildings. It is informed largely, although not wholly, by the dimensional criteria in the British Standard 8300:2001 *Design of buildings and their approaches to meet the needs of disabled people – Code of practice*, see p 7. Where there are differences in the dimensional or other criteria, these result from accumulated experience fed back to the Government during the consultation process for the new AD M. The guidance in

AD M should be followed in preference to the criteria in BS 8300. It is important that reference is made to AD M for details of the circumstances in which Part M applies and what provision is required.

Scotland

On 1 May 2005 a new building standards system comes into force in Scotland. The Building (Scotland) Act 2003 gives Scottish Ministers the power to make building regulations which will be administered by the Scottish Building Standards Agency (SBSA), a new executive agency of the Scottish Executive.

The building standards are supported by two new Technical Handbooks: a Domestic Handbook and a Non-domestic Handbook. The Handbooks provide guidance on achieving the standards set in the Building (Scotland) Regulations 2004. Access requirements are integrated into the Technical Handbooks, as they were in the previous Technical Standards.

Northern Ireland

In Northern Ireland, Part R of the Building Regulations (NI) covers *Access and Facilities for Disabled People*, and is supported by Technical Booklet R:2000.

Disability Discrimination Act 1995

The Disability Discrimination Act (DDA) introduced new measures aimed at ending the discrimination which many disabled people face. In addition to granting new rights to disabled people, the Act also places duties on, among others, employers (Part 2), providers of goods, facilities and services (Part 3) and education providers (Part 4).

The main thrust of the legislation is to improve access for disabled people to employment, education and services. While the DDA does not directly require accessible environments to be provided for disabled people, either in their place of work or for access to goods, facilities, or services (for example in shops, restaurants or offices to which the public have access), duties under the Act include the requirement to consider barriers created by physical features of buildings and to make adjustments in certain circumstances.

The Act defines a disabled person as 'someone who has a physical or mental impairment which has a substantial and long-term adverse effect on his or her ability to carry out normal day-to-day activities'. Discrimination occurs where without justification, and for a reason which relates to the disabled person's disability, a disabled person is treated less favourably than others to whom the reason does not or would not apply. Discrimination may also occur when there is a duty to make a reasonable adjustment, and any failure to meet that duty cannot be justified.

Each Part of the DDA is supported by one or more Codes of Practice which give guidance on how to meet duties under the Act. While Codes of Practice neither impose legal obligations nor are authoritative statements of the law, they may be referred to in any legal proceedings pursued under the Act. Building designers, while not legally required to respond to the DDA, should anticipate the requirements of the Act by presuming that employees, students and customers will fit the definition of 'disabled person' under the Act, and design buildings accordingly. Those commissioning new buildings or adaptations to existing buildings should consider the implications of the DDA in terms of their ability to employ and offer services to disabled people on an equal basis.

The DDA applies to the whole of the UK, including (with modifications) Northern Ireland.

DDA Part 2: Employment

Employers have a duty not to treat disabled people less favourably than others for a reason relating to their disability, unless this can be justified, and to make adjustments to assist disabled employees or applicants for employment. This may involve changing physical features of the premises if these put a disabled person at a substantial disadvantage in comparison with persons who are not disabled. The duty of provision of a reasonable adjustment is triggered when an individual disabled person applies for a job, is employed, or it becomes apparent that an existing employee requires some form of adjustment; there is no general or anticipatory duty under Part 2 to make provision for disabled people.

Duties in Part 2 of the DDA covering employers were introduced in December 1996 and have subsequently been amended under the Equal Treatment Directive, which implements obligations placed by the European Union on the UK in relation to disability discrimination. From 1 October 2004, the Directive brought into effect the removal of the existing exemption for small employers so that the Part 2 duties relate to all employers. The Directive has also changed the relationship between the Building Regulations and Part 2 of the DDA. The partial exemption from the duty to remove or alter physical features which applies to service providers under Part 3 of the Act no longer applies to employers under Part 2.

DDA Part 3: Service provision

Part 3 of the DDA places duties on those providing goods, facilities or services to the public ('service providers') and those selling, letting or managing premises. The Act makes it unlawful for service providers, landlords and other persons to discriminate against disabled people in certain circumstances.

The duties on service providers have been introduced in three stages:

- Since December 1996, it has been unlawful for service providers to treat disabled people less favourably for a reason related to their disability.
- Since October 1999, service providers have had to make 'reasonable adjustments' for disabled people, such as providing extra help or making changes to the way they provide their services, or overcoming physical barriers by providing a service by a reasonable alternative method.
- From October 2004, service providers may have to make other 'reasonable

adjustments' in relation to the physical features of their premises to overcome physical barriers to access.

The *Code of Practice Rights of Access: Goods, Facilities, Services and Premises*, published by the Disability Rights Commission in 2002, outlines what may be considered as reasonable for disabled people to establish rights of access to goods, facilities, services and premises. Several factors have a bearing on whether a change is a reasonable one to make: effectiveness; practicality; cost and disruption; and financial resources.

DDA Part 4: Education

The Special Educational Needs and Disability Act 2001 (SENDA) amended Part 4 of the DDA and expanded the duties relating to disabled pupils and students. Education providers are now required to make 'reasonable adjustments' for disabled students and pupils. The duties cover all areas of education, schools, colleges, universities, adult education and youth services, including:

- not to treat disabled students or pupils less favourably than non-disabled students or pupils without justification
- to make reasonable adjustments to policies, practices and procedures that may discriminate against disabled students or pupils
- to provide education by a 'reasonable alternative means' where a physical feature places a disabled student/pupil at a substantial disadvantage
- a duty on local education authorities in England and Wales to plan strategically and increase the overall accessibility to school premises and the curriculum (a similar duty is placed on authorities in Scotland under the Education (Disability Strategies and Pupils' Education Records) (Scotland) Act 2002)

Additional duties placed on providers of post-16 education are as follows:

- from September 2002: not to discriminate against existing and prospective disabled students by treating them less favourably in the provision of student services

- from September 2003: to make reasonable adjustments to provide auxiliary aids
- from September 2005: to make adjustments to physical features. This is an anticipatory and continuing duty

Many schools or further/higher education providers are also service providers (for example where premises are used for evening classes, exhibitions or parents' evenings), and therefore also have duties under Part 3.

Sources of useful information

Organisations

British Standards Institution (BSI)
389 Chiswick High Road
London W4 4AL
Tel: 020 8996 9000
Fax: 020 8996 7001
Email: cservices@bsi-global. com
Website: www.bsi.org.uk

Publishes British Standards including BS 8300:2001 *Design of buildings and their approaches to meet the needs of disabled people – Code of practice.*

Centre for Accessible Environments
70 South Lambeth Road
London SW8 1RL
Tel/textphone: 020 7840 0125
Fax: 020 7840 5811
Email: info@cae.org.uk
Website: www.cae.org.uk

Provides technical information, training and consultancy on making buildings accessible to all users, including disabled and older people and carers of young children.

Construction Products Association
26 Store Street
London WC1E 7BT
Tel: 020 7323 3770
Fax: 020 7323 0307
Email: enquiries@constprod.org.uk
Website: www.constprod.org.uk

Trade association representing manufacturers and suppliers of construction products, components and fittings.

Department of Finance and Personnel
Building Regulations Unit
Third Floor, Lancashire House
3 Linenhall Street
Belfast BT2 8AA
Tel: 028 9054 2923
Email: DFP.enquiries@dfpni.gov.uk
Website: www2.dfpni.gov.uk

For information on the Northern Ireland Technical Booklets.

Disability Rights Commission
DRC Helpline
Freepost MID 02164
Stratford-upon-Avon CV37 9BR
Tel: 08457 622 633
Textphone: 08457 622 644
Fax: 08457 778 878
Email: enquiry@drc-gb.org
Website: www.drc.org.uk

Publishes codes of practice and other guidance related to the DDA.

The Equality Commission for Northern Ireland
Equality House
7–9 Shaftesbury Square
Belfast BT2 7DP
Tel: 028 90 500600
Fax: 028 90 248687
Textphone: 028 90 500589
Email: information@equalityni.org

Works towards the elimination of discrimination and keeps the relevant legislation under review.

Guild of Architectural Ironmongers
8 Stepney Green
London E1 3JU
Tel: 020 7790 3431
Fax: 020 7790 8517
Email: info@gai.org.uk
Website: www.gai.org.uk

Technical information and advice. Guidance on changes in legislation, regulations and standards affecting fire and escape door hardware.

Royal Institute of British Architects (RIBA)
66 Portland Place
London W1B 1AD
Public information line: 0906 302 0400
Tel: 020 7580 5533
Fax: 020 7255 1541
Email: info@inst.riba.org
Website: www.architecture.com

The RIBA advances architecture by demonstrating benefit to society and excellence in the profession.

Scottish Building Standards Agency
Denholm House
Almondvale Business Park
Livingston EH54 6GA
Tel: 01506 600 400
Fax: 01506 600 401
Email: info@sbsa.gov.uk
Website: www.sbsa.gov.uk

For information on the Scottish Technical Handbooks.

The Stationery Office Ltd
PO Box 29
Duke Street
Norwich NR3 1GN
Tel: 0870 600 5522
Fax: 0870 600 5533
Email: services@tso.co.uk
Online ordering:
www. tso.co.uk/bookshop

Sells printed versions of any item of legislation or any other official publication previously published by HMSO.

Publications

Legislation, standards and codes of practice

The Building Regulations 2000 Approved Document M: Access to and use of buildings (England and Wales)
Office of the Deputy Prime Minister
The Stationery Office, 2003

The Building Regulations (Northern Ireland) 2000 Technical booklet R: Access and facilities for disabled people
Great Britain Department of Finance and Personnel (Northern Ireland)
The Stationery Office, 2001

Non-Domestic Technical Handbook
Scottish Executive
The Stationery Office, 2005

BS 8300:2001 Design of buildings and their approaches to meet the needs of disabled people – Code of practice
British Standards Institution, 2001

Code of Practice Rights of Access to Goods, Facilities, Services and Premises
Disability Rights Commission
The Stationery Office, 2002

Code of Practice for providers of Post-16 education and related services
Disability Rights Commission
The Stationery Office, 2002

Code of Practice for Schools
Disability Rights Commission
The Stationery Office, 2002

Code of Practice – Employment and Occupation
Disability Rights Commission
The Stationery Office, 2004

Code of Practice – Trade Organisations and Qualification Bodies
Disability Rights Commission
The Stationery Office, 2004

Other publications

Access for Disabled People
Sport England, 2002
Design guidance note including a series of checklists for auditing sports buildings.

Building Sight
by Peter Barker, Jon Barrick, Rod Wilson
HMSO in association with the Royal National
Institute of the Blind
RNIB, 1995
A handbook of building and interior design
solutions to include the needs of visually
impaired people.

Designing for Accessibility
CAE/RIBA Enterprises, 2004
Up-to-date and user-friendly good practice
guide based on the 2004 Approved Document
M and BS 8300:2001

**A Design Guide for the Use of Colour and
Contrast to Improve the Built Environment for
Visually Impaired People**
Dulux Technical Group, ICI Paints, 1997

**Disabled Access to Facilities: A practical and
comprehensive guide to a service provider's
duties under Part III (2004) of the Disability
Discrimination Act 1995
FM Law Series**
by Ian Waterman and Janet A Bell,
Access Matters UK Ltd
Butterworths Tolley Lexis Nexis, 2002

Good Loo Design Guide
CAE/RIBA Enterprises, 2004
Authoritative design guidance on WCs that
meet the requirement of all users.

**Inclusive School Design – Accommodating
pupils with special educational needs and
disabilities in mainstream schools**
Department for Education and Employment
The Stationery Office, 2001

Sign Design Guide
by Peter Parker and June Fraser
JMU and the Sign Design Society, 2000
A guide to inclusive signage